Learn To Draw
Girls Pencil Drawings
Step by Step

Figure Drawing Books for Absolute Beginners

By Gala Publication

PUBLISHED BY:

Gala Publication

ISBN-13: 978- 1508673576
ISBN-10: 1508673578

©Copyright 2015 – Gala Publication

Table Of Content :

Steampunk-Girl

Step1

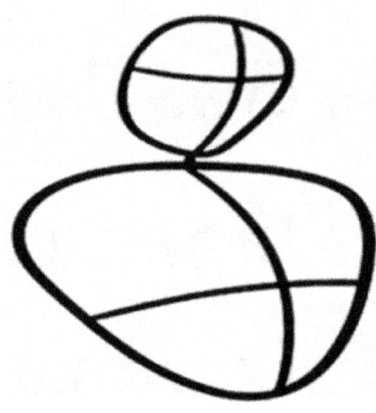

Step2

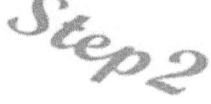

Step3

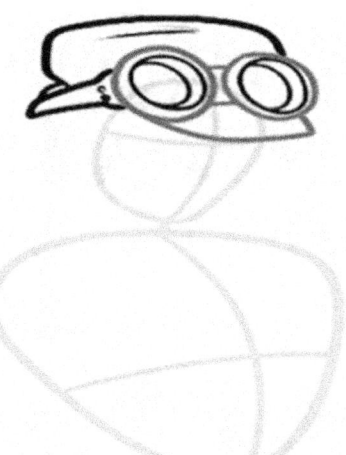

Step4

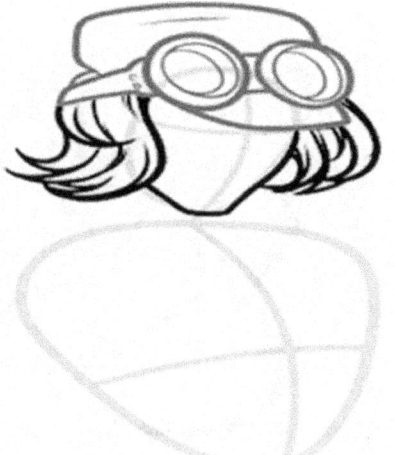

Step 5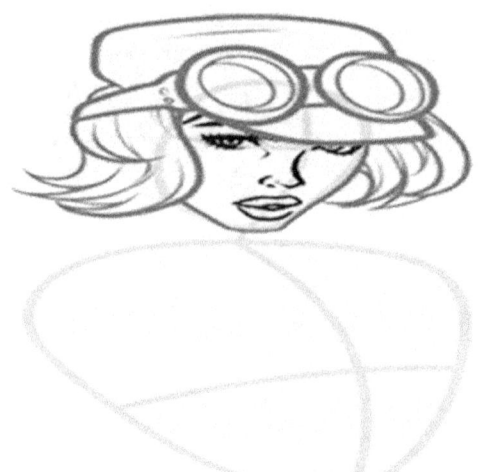

Step 6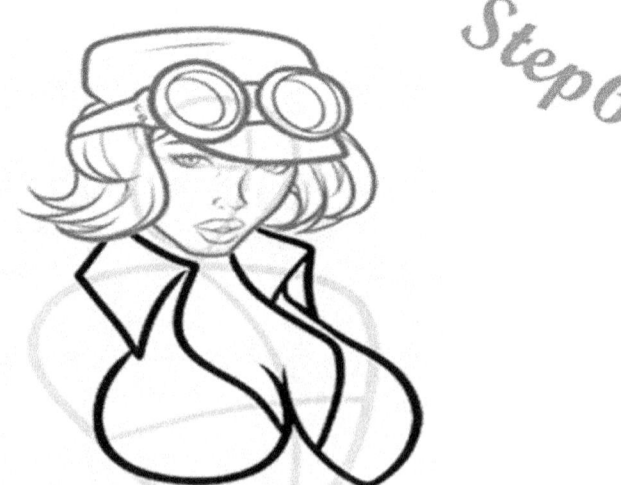

Step7

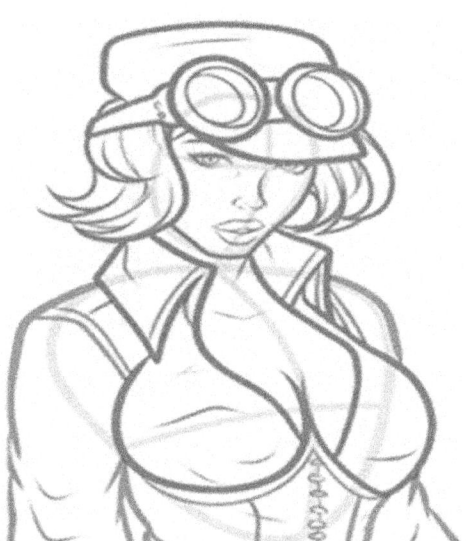

Step8

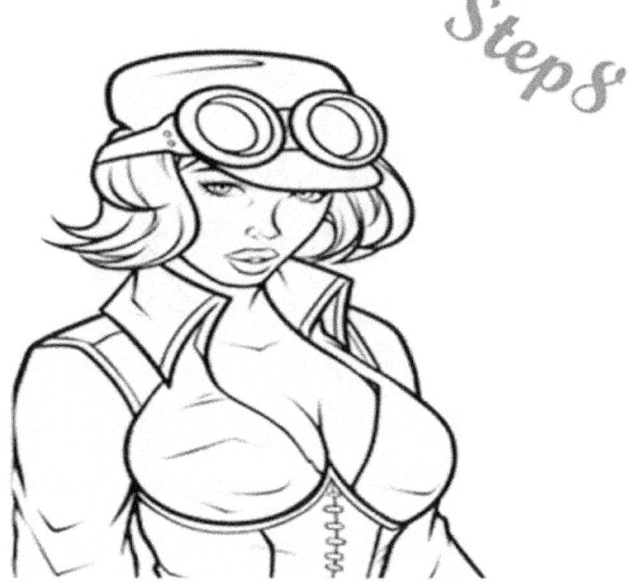

Cowgirl

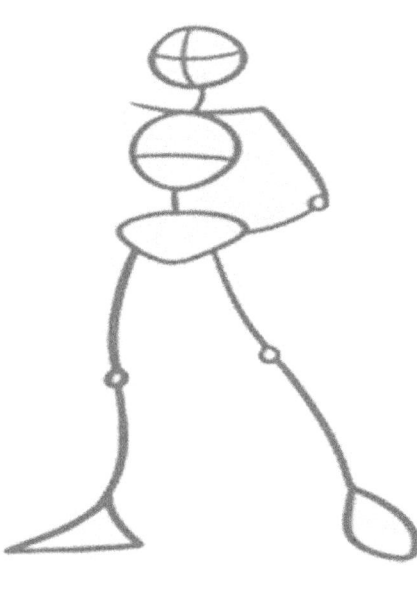

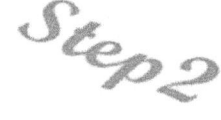

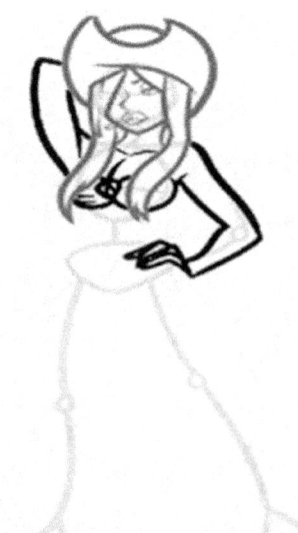

Step3

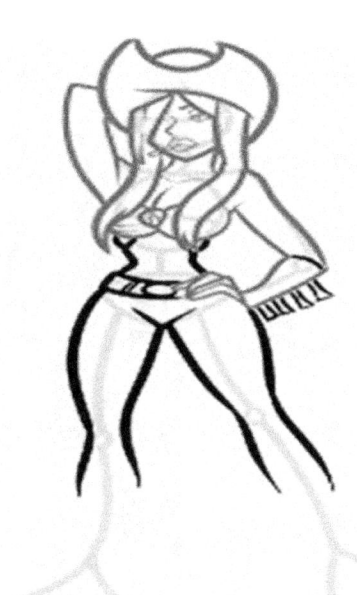

Step4

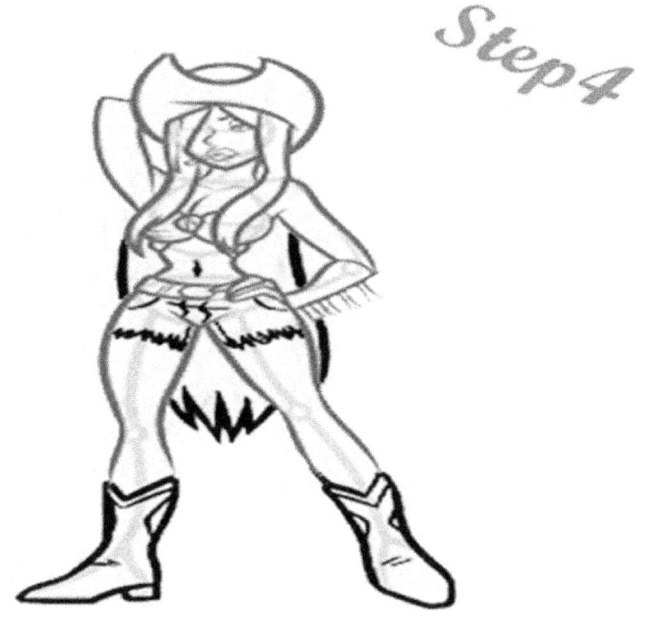

Step 5

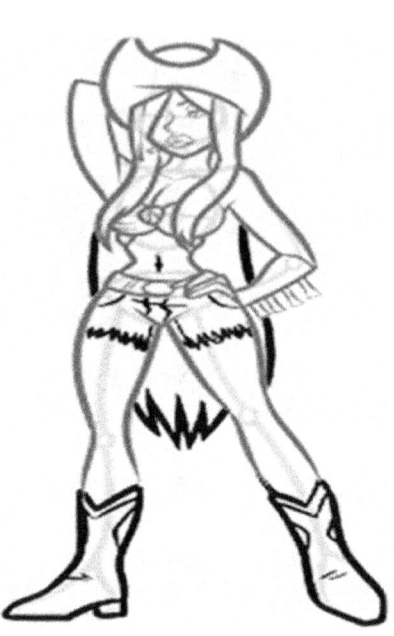

Step 6

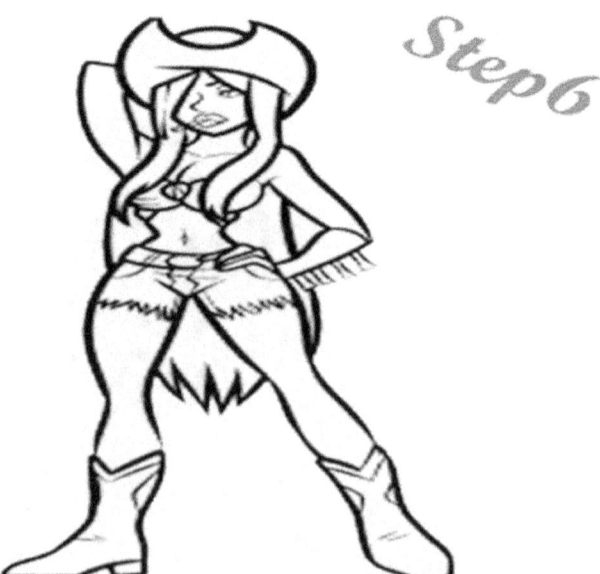

Maid

Step1

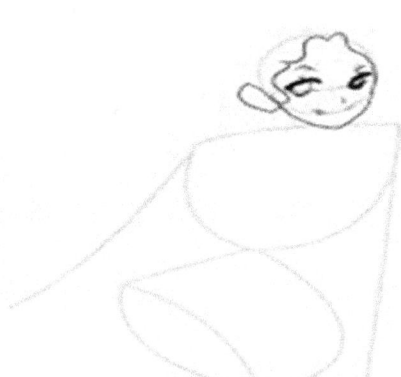

Step2

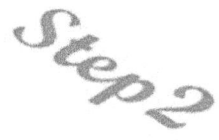

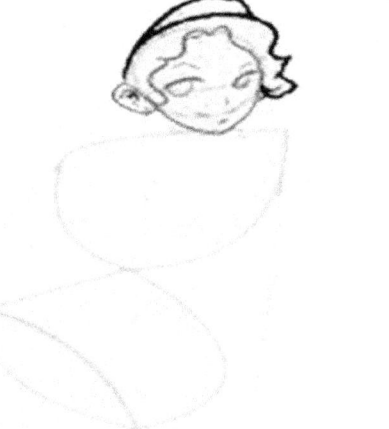

Step3

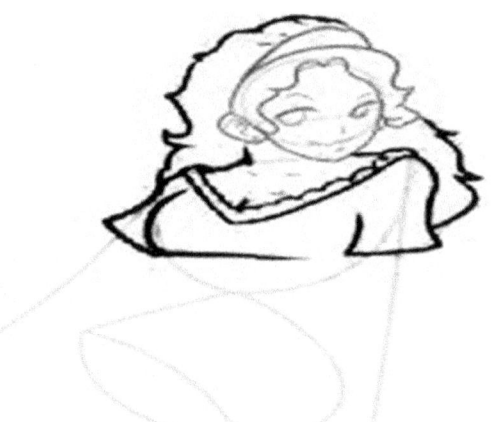

Step4

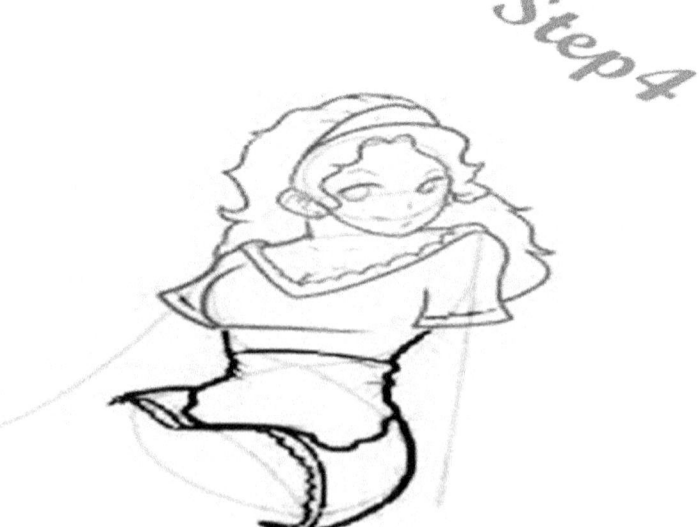

Step 5

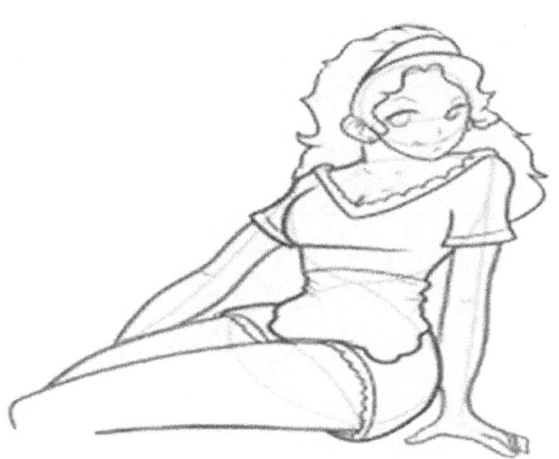

Step 6

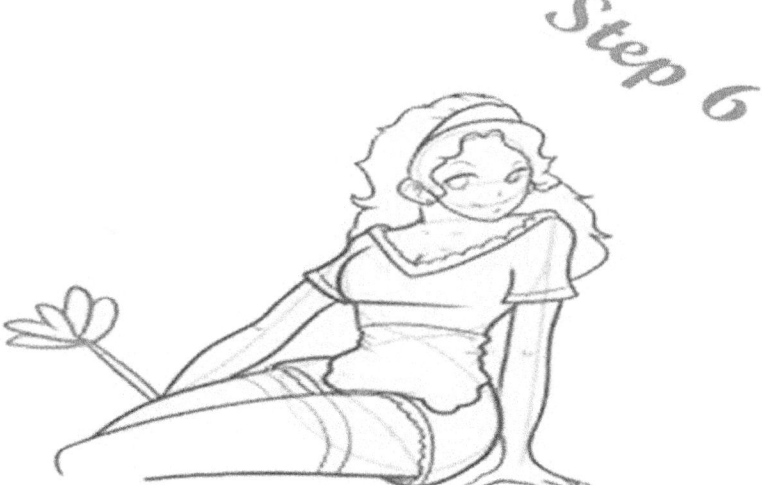

Step 7

Step 8

Scene-Girls

Step1

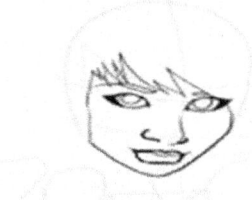

Step 2

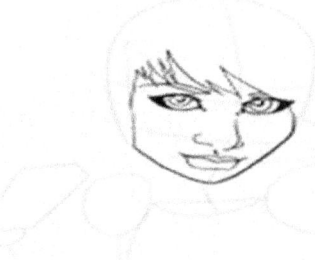

Step 3

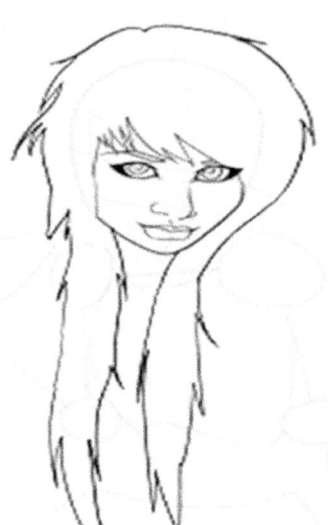

Step 4

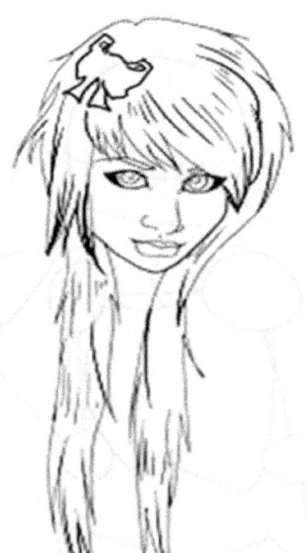

Step 5

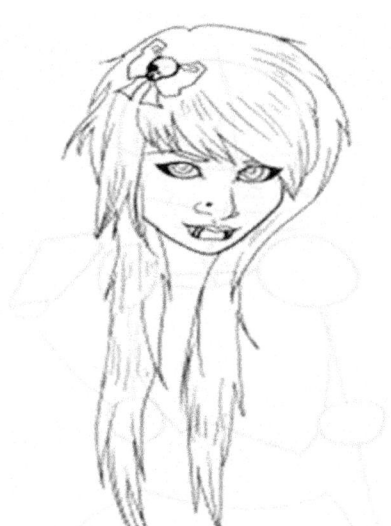

Step 6

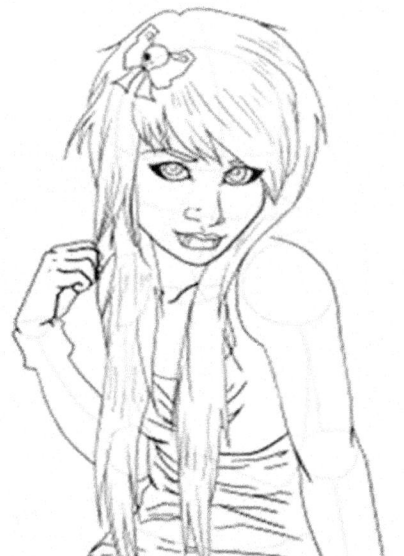

Step7

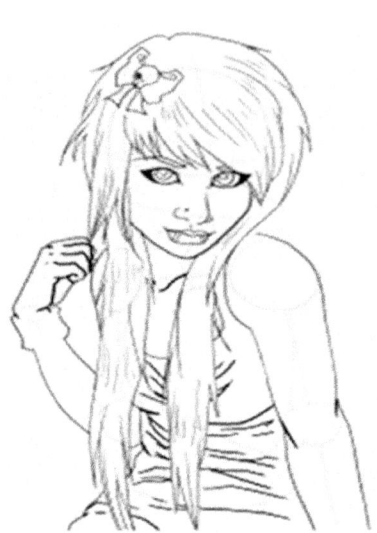

Step 8

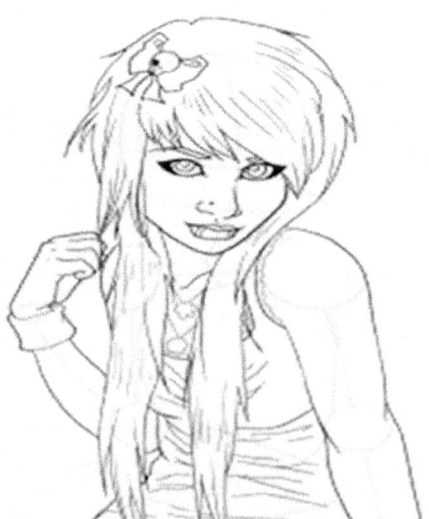

Emo-Girls

Step 1

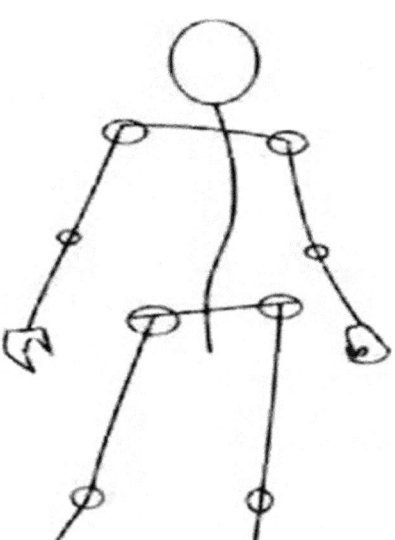

Step 2

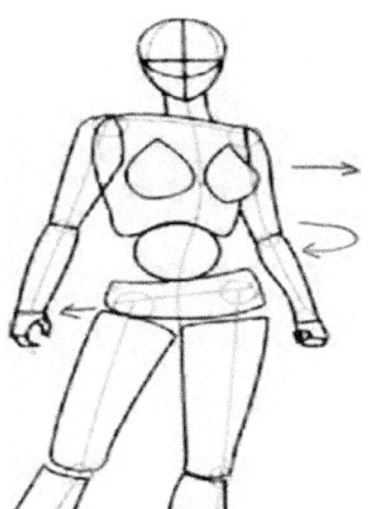

Step 3

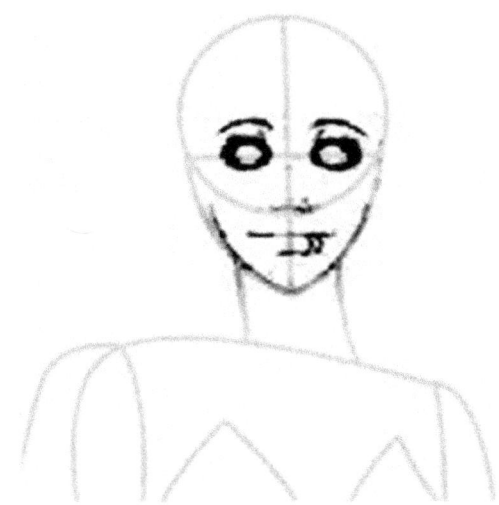

Step 4

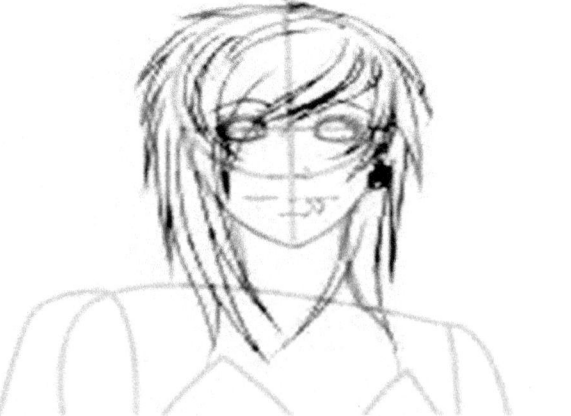

Step 5

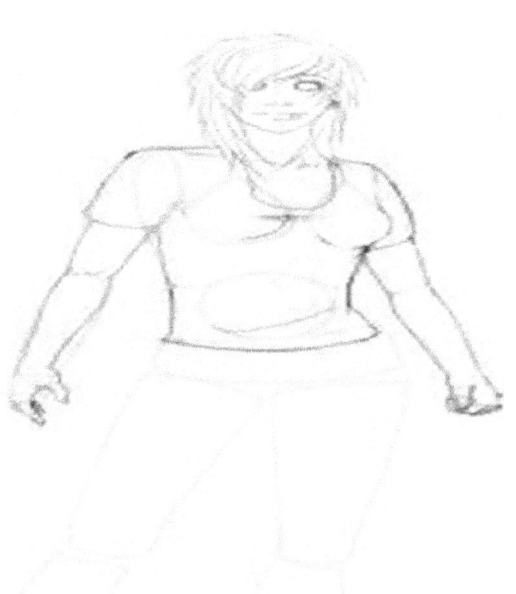

Step 6

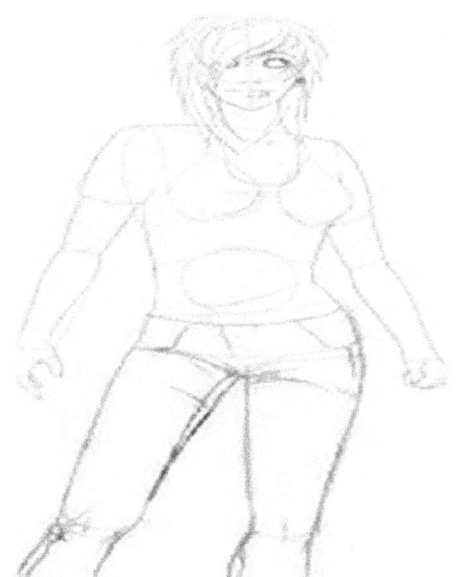

Step7

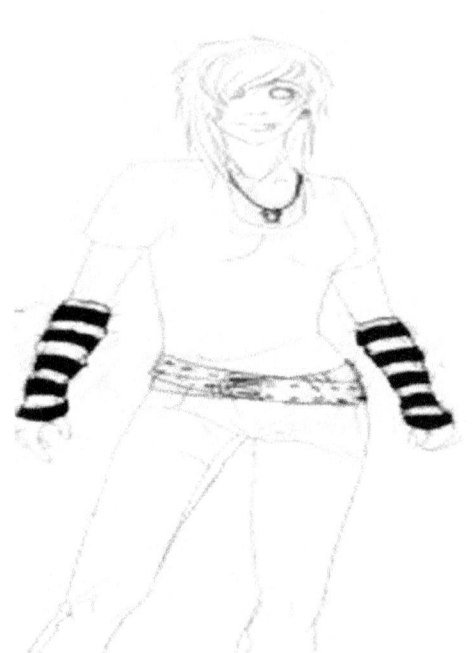

Step 8

Anime-girl

Step1

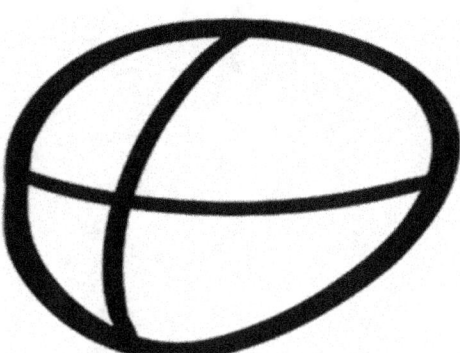

Step 2

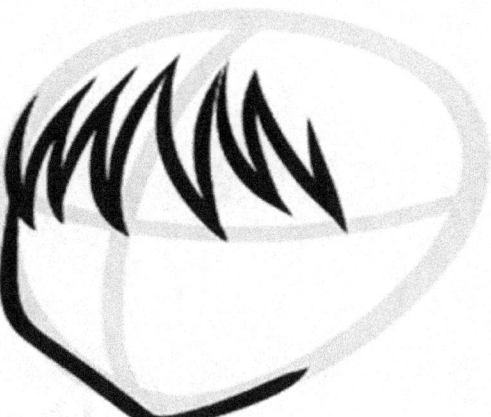

Step3

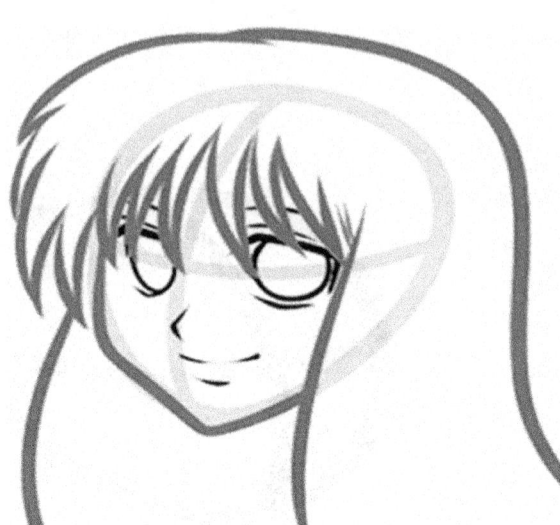

Step 4

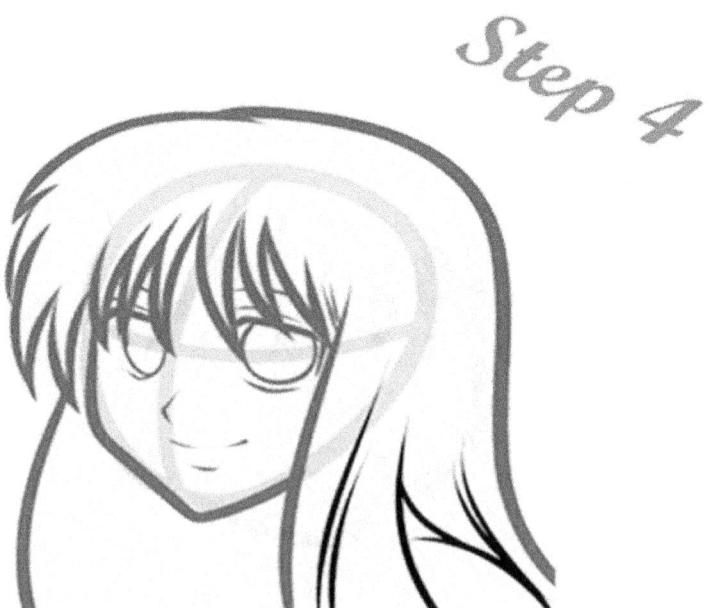

Step 5

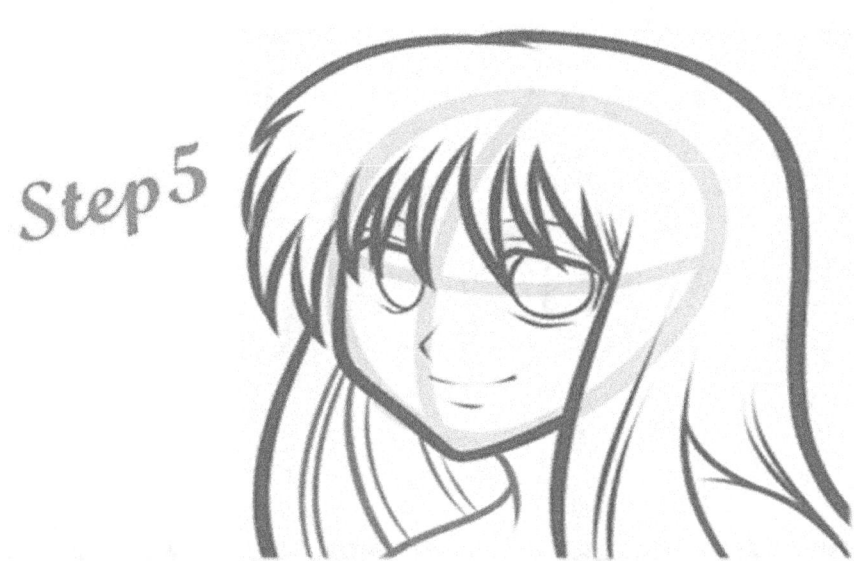

Step 6

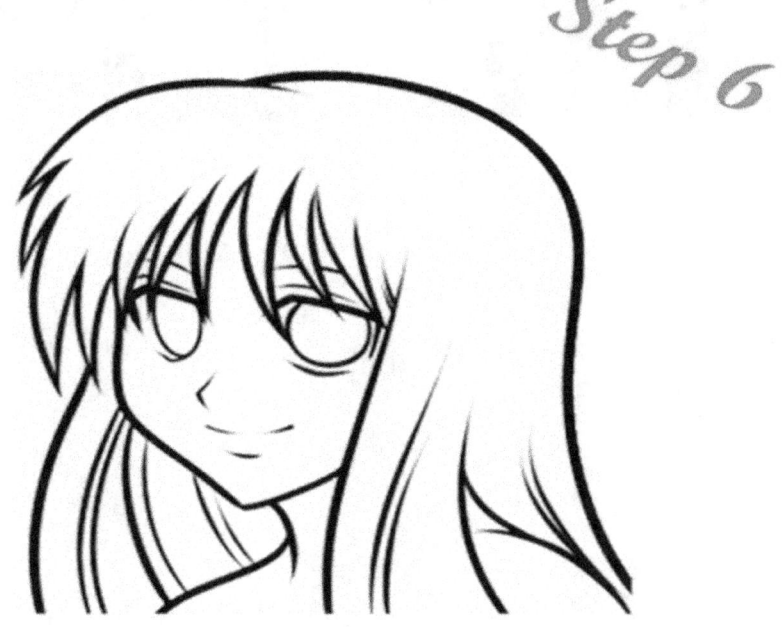

THE END